Big Machines in the Military

by Brienna Rossiter

www.focusreaders.com

Focus Readers is distributed by North Star Editions:
sales@northstareditions.com | 888-417-0195

Produced for Focus Readers by Red Line Editorial.

Photographs ©: Shutterstock Images, cover, 1, 4, 7 (top), 7 (bottom), 9, 11 (top), 11 (bottom), 13, 15 (top), 15 (bottom), 16 (top left), 16 (top right), 16 (bottom left), 16 (bottom right)

Library of Congress Cataloging-in-Publication Data
Names: Rossiter, Brienna, author.
Title: Big machines in the military / by Brienna Rossiter.
Description: Lake Elmo, MN : Focus Readers, [2021] | Series: Big machines | Includes index. | Audience: Grades K-1.
Identifiers: LCCN 2020033511 (print) | LCCN 2020033512 (ebook) | ISBN 9781644936733 (hardcover) | ISBN 9781644937099 (paperback) | ISBN 9781644937815 (ebook pdf) | ISBN 9781644937457 (hosted ebook)
Subjects: LCSH: Airplanes, Military--Juvenile literature. | Tanks--Juvenile literature. | Warships--Juvenile literature.
Classification: LCC UG1240 .R67 2021 (print) | LCC UG1240 (ebook) | DDC 623.74--dc23
LC record available at https://lccn.loc.gov/2020033511
LC ebook record available at https://lccn.loc.gov/2020033512

Printed in the United States of America
Mankato, MN
012021

About the Author

Brienna Rossiter is a writer and editor who lives in Minnesota. She loves being outside and traveling in airplanes.

Table of Contents

track

On the Ground

Tanks fight on land.

Tanks roll on **tracks**.

Tanks shoot big guns.

In the Air

Helicopters fly.

They carry **soldiers**.

The soldiers jump out.

helicopter

soldier

Planes fly, too.

Some planes are fighters.

They fly fast.

They shoot.

fighter

Some planes are bombers.

They drop **bombs**.

The bombs blow up.

In the Water

Ships go on water.

Some ships fight.

They have many guns.

Some ships hold planes.

Planes land on the ships.

They take off, too.

plane

Glossary

bombs

soldiers

helicopters

tracks

Index